The People's History
Annfield Plain
& District

by Jack Hair

Alan McNeill and Ronnie George with a Co-op Diary horse and cart at a show in the early 1950s. They delivered to Kyo, East Stanley, South Stanley and Quaking Houses.

Previous page: The Annfield Plain village blacksmith.

Copyright © Jack Hair 2002

First published in 2002 by

The People's History Ltd
Suite 1
Byron House
Seaham Grange Business Park
Seaham
Co. Durham
SR7 0PY

ISBN 1 902527 83 6

Contents

Atkinson's Fruit Market, West Road.

The demolition of Atkinson's Fruit Market in November 1988.

Introduction

Other books have been compiled on this area by people like Fred Wade and Bill Jennings. They are a more accurate historical and factual account than I could hope to do. Their books are available in the local libraries and are a worthy read for students of the subject. I have drawn from their great knowledge of the area.

I hope to give a more personal recollection of people's memories, plus an insight into the life of the district by way of photographs, and a reflection on people's memories as they recall them.

Annfield Plain is situated in North Durham and owes its existence mostly due to the coalmining industry. Although there has been coalmining down several centuries in the area, the growth of the town can mostly be identified with the opening of the deep coalmines from the mid eighteen hundreds.

Coalmining has long gone, but the people remain, and it is my belief that the strength of any district, is the people. Let's hope this book is a 'People's History'.

I would also reiterate that the book is only as accurate as people's memories. It is not intended as a reference book.

J. Reece, Newsagents and General Dealer, Catherine Terrace, New Kyo.

Annfield Plain Library Reading Room Committee of 1951. Included are: Mr Fred Wade, Miss E. Trowsdale, Mr V. Richards, J.T.C. Hall, Mrs I. Bell, Mr E. Tucker, Mr J.W. Lawson, Mr W. Simpson, Mr C. Warren, Mr J. Atkinson, Mr J. Pigg and Mr J. Finney. The library has recently been refurbished and is still well used today.

Acknowledgements

Mr Alan Harrison, who, but for the pressure of work, would have been co-author. I thank him for his contributions.

Adrian Hair, my son for his help and interest, Mr & Mrs T. Harris, Mrs Thew, Douglas & Genia Collin, J. Goodwin Jnr, Mr & Mrs Hylton Marrs, Marshall Lawson, Norman Taylor, Terry Fenwick, Norman Wilkinson, Mick Horswill and family, Glenn McCrory and family, PC Ian Ward, R. Greener, Sheila Forster, Mr Beckham, Keith & Colin McPhail, Mr Joel, Miss Tullet, Bob Drake, Clare Williams, the County Library Service, the landlords and committees of the local pubs and clubs, church leaders, head teachers, fellow local historians, Gadgetman Productions, the Resource Centre at Beamish Museum – who assure me many of these photos are available at Beamish – and so many more who have helped and given of their time. Even if I have not included your name, your assistance has been invaluable.

Most of all, I dedicate this book to my wife Margaret for her great support.

Kindest regards
Jack Hair

AROUND
ANNFIELD PLAIN

A view towards the junction of West Road and Front Street with Pontop Pike
Television Mast in the distance.

Horse drawn traffic passing the Co-operative Store on the right and Station Buildings on the left.

A 1930s view of Annfield Plain Park, showing the lake and bandstand. Also showing is the Railway Station footbridge. The land on which this park is now situated was originally woodland. This area eventually became controlled by the South Moor Coal Company and the road into the woodland area, once private, was opened to the public. The trees were felled for use during the First World War. In 1919, the Coal Company offered the land to Annfield Plain Urban District Council to form a park of approximately 14 acres, free of charge. During the 1921 Depression, they used laid off miners and others out of work to build the new park. Once completed, it was officially opened on Saturday, 12th July 1923 by Mr T.Y. Greener, agent for the South Moor Coal Co. Several hundred people attended this ceremony and they were later entertained by the local colliery band. The bowling green and sports pavilion were added in September 1936.

A 1950s view down West Road.

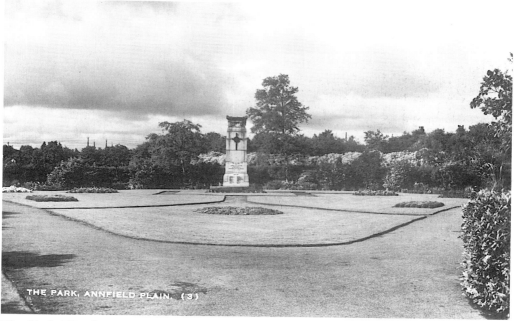

The Park War Memorial. The memorial was unveiled on Sunday 25th April 1925 by the Earl of Durham. It bears the following inscription: 'To Our Glorious Dead. A symbol of Gratitude to the men of Annfield Plain, who died in the defence of Freedom and the Empire 1914-1918.' The names of the fallen are on the stone with: 'To him that overcometh, will give the Crown of Life.' This memorial was erected by Messrs A.F. Manuelle of London. After the Second World War, further names were added.

South Pontop War Memorial. This is situated in the Avenue at Greencroft. The memorial was erected by the owners, officials and workmen of South Pontop Colliery with the inscription: 'In memory of our village comrades who fell in the Great War 1914-1918.' It also reads: 'The Blood of Heroes is the Seed of Freedom.' It was unveiled on the 27th May 1920. Even though this memorial is in a prominent position, many local people are not aware of its existence.

The Loud Bank Memorial to Pilot Sergeant Martin Joyce. In March 1918, a plane crashed on Loud Bank and burst into flames opposite Loud Terrace. This resulted in the death of Pilot Sergeant Joyce of the Royal Flying Corps. Public donations, mostly raised by local children, paid for the memorial, costing £50. His memorial has the crest of the Royal Flying Corps and the inscription: 'It was here that Martin Joyce, Air Pilot, met his death on 13th March 1918. This monument is erected by the inhabitants of Annfield Plain & District in recognition of the gallant airman's great sacrifice. In his own words 'Our lives are not our own. They belong to our country.' The crash was witnessed by Mr E. Carr of Loud Terrace. The iron surround was removed during the Second World War and replaced by the block of stone on which the monument now stands. It reads: 'Dedicated May 14th 1919. It was renovated and re Dedicated on 12th February 1959. Ornamental surrounds were erected by West Stanley RAFA in memory of all ranks of the RAF during the war. WE Will Remember Them.' It was unveiled by Air Marshall, Sir Geoffrey Bromel, KBE CB DSO on 12th July 1959.

The Women's Institute

Annfield Plain WI Hall above the shops in West Road 1989. The Annfield Plain Women's Institute was first registered on 15th February 1930. The first president was Mrs W. Jackson. The meetings were held in the library and then in the Liberal Hut which was situated between the garage and Field House, opposite South View. On 11th May 1931, they held their first group meeting at St Aidan's Hall which then stood on the site of the present day doctor's surgery at Annfield Plain. They formed a drama group and choir and, on Wednesday, 20th April 1932, these two groups united to give a concert entitled 'The Neighbours of Sunshine Valley' admission 6d.

The drama group and choir. Included are: Mrs Thompson, Miss Hayton, Mrs White, Mrs Hodgson, Mrs Watchman, Mrs Maddison, Mrs Crisp Snr, Mrs Spears, Mrs Parker, Miss Williams, Mrs Fisk, Miss Todd, Mrs Ledger, Mrs Crisp Jnr, Mrs Watchman, Miss Stansfield, Jack Thompson, Cyril Maddison and Ron Thompson. In 1937, the choir were presented with a cup by the county president, Mrs Lloyd Pease.

In 1938, the WI rented part of the premises in West Road from the Annfield Plain Freemasons. During the Second World War, the hall was used by the YMCA for troops stationed in the area. Special Constables also used the room free of charge. The WI provided tea and entertainment. By 1944, the troops were drafted away to the Second Front. At this time, the president asked the Masonic Authority permission to use the rooms vacated by the YMCA. In 1946, the Freemasons decided to sell the complete premises to the WI at a cost of £1,100 and a deposit of 10%. The sale was completed on 14th March 1949 when the WI paid £250 and took out a mortgage for the balance. The 25th Anniversary was celebrated with a dinner dance for the members. Mrs J. Armstrong represented the Annfield Plain WI at a Royal Garden Party held in London. The 50th Anniversary was celebrated with a dinner dance held at the Iveston Hotel on the 15th February 1980. For many years they held dinner dances at Castle's Ballroom, Catchgate. The longest serving president of the Annfield Plain WI was Mrs Ardron, November 1961-May 1986.

Past presidents were:

1930	Mrs Jackson
1931	Mrs Trowsdale
1933	Mrs Roberts
1934	Mrs Hutton
1938	Mrs Horsefield
1942	Mrs Beattie
1947	Mrs Sheraton
1948	Mrs Maddison
1953	Mrs White
1957	Mrs Bulmer
1960	Mrs White
1961	Mrs Ardron
1986	Mrs Collin

Most of this information is from Mrs Collin's 'President's Address' to the members at the time of their 60th Anniversary held on 15th February 1990. The Women's Institute in Annfield Plain is still active today but they no longer use the premises in West Road. Meetings have been held in Annfield Plain Library since 30th February 1996.

Mrs Collin, WI President, cutting the cake at the WI's 65th birthday party.

Below: The Annfield Plain WI garden party at Harperley in 1930.

Annfield House. This is believed to be one of the oldest houses in Annfield Plain and is situated at the top of the Loud Bank. This was a farmhouse and is still standing today. The house was built some time before 1778. The first tenant was Mr Peacock who named the house in honour of his wife Ann. The land surrounding the house was known as 'Ann's Fields', hence Annfield. The first mention is in 1778, in the Lanchester Parish Records. The name 'Plane' was due to the engine plane (a standing engine) of the Stanhope & Tyne Railway Co which was used to haul wagons up the Loud. The name changed to Plain in 1885.

East Castle. East Castle was known originally as 'Bantling Castle'. This village took its name from the nearby lime kilns of the Stanhope & Tyne Railway Co. The kilns resembled castles. The name 'Bantling' was supposedly due to the small stature of the miners who came to work at one of the pits in the village. Most of the village was demolished in 1957 with only the former East Castle pub and a few houses built originally for railway workers remaining.

The East Castle Inn was the second pub in the village, the first one being demolished. It is now the home of Mr & Mrs Heron.

East Castle Street. This is the last street remaining in the former mining village. It was originally named Railway Cottages. These houses are now owned by Mrs Wilson who has traded as Northumbria Horse Riding Holidays for over 20 years.

W. Thew's General Dealers
– Mrs Thew with staff,
Amelia Liddle and Doreen.
William and Elleanor Thew
traded as General Dealers at
New Kyo from 1950-1971.
Mr Thew also had a milk
delivery business which he
enlarged over the years. He
much preferred the outdoor
work to that of the shop.
When they retired, the shop
was sold to Mr & Mrs
Maurice Clish, who
themselves ran the business
until 2001.

Annie Hutchinson, Nellie
Mason and Doreen Thew,
daughter of Mr & Mrs Thew.

Prospect Terrace, New Kyo, 1924. This is believed to have been Littlefair's shop. The bus stop opposite is still known locally today as Littlefair's.

The shop of Andrew (Ante) Harris at Prospect Terrace in the early 1920s. Note the early adverts of the day: Colman's Starch, Wills' Gold Flake, Cadbury's, Oxo, Bournville Chocolate, Player's Navy Cut and Brooke Bond Tea. The Harris family traded in New Kyo and Annfield Plain for over 60 years. Andrew Harris was followed by his sons Bill and later Vernie, who took over the business in the 1930s. They traded in the shop shown until 1985.

Harris's Stores in 1958 with Maureen Curran, Rita Dodds and Olive Harris. This shop resembled the shop on TV, 'Open All Hours', in so much as it sold everything you could need from a general dealers.

Vernie Harris' Shop, 1954. Outside the shop are: Edna Burnage, Olive Harris and Marion Kerr. Pictured in the van is dog Laddie. In the early 1970s, Vernie was badly injured when a delivery van accidentally reversed over him outside the shop.

Harris's Superette, Annfield Plain, 1963. This shop was opened by Vernie Harris' son Tom and his wife Ethel. They were very modern in their thoughts as this was one of the first shops of its kind in the district, offering a totally new concept in shopping, 'the supermarket'.

Tom and Ethel Harris standing proudly in their new supermarket at Annfield Plain. Note the pre-decimal prices. The family also had the café at Prospect Terrace, New Kyo, in the early 1950s, in what was originally Littlefair's. Florrie Thwaites managed the café with Polly until 1953. They supposedly did a grand three course meal for 2/6d old money. Tom and Ethel traded in New Kyo until 1985 and they still live in the area.

Mr Mitchieson pictured at his home, which was built by the Claverings, situated opposite the south side of Ransome & Marles Factory.

A very rare photograph of a wooden house with slated roof, formerly on the site, at the west end, of what was Ransome & Marles at Greencroft.

Hare Law Garage. Ray Barnett acquired the old premises of Rington's and then went on to erect the garage shown in the picture. He has traded on this site since 1957 and was the first Esso garage in the area to fit the new display pumps. To the right of the garage is a short street of houses (no longer standing) which were named after the former owners of the surrounding land, Oxley. In that street was Mrs Lumley's shop. In the left foreground of the photo is the churchyard of St Thomas' Church. Behind the garage is the housing estate and, on the horizon, you can see two pit chimneys. This photo was taken from the Hare Law Pit Heaps.

West Road, leading from Annfield Plain up to Greencroft, showing several early shops plus the site of the original Coach & Horses. The colliery headgear of the Hutton Pit is just visible.

Pontop Rows. These old cottages, shown from the railway crossings, were erected originally by the Railway Company for their workers. They were later used as homes for the coalminers and their families. To call them homes is probably an exaggeration as they were very basic indeed, with raw sewage running down channels between the streets of houses. The miners' families suffered many deaths from diseases living in such poor quality accommodation.

Wood Rows. The Wood Rows in Clavering Place, were built for coal owner, John Dickinson of the Bankfoot Pit. The houses were laid out in rows, and were described in 1872, in the *Newcastle Weekly Chronicle*, according to John Griffiths, as merely 'Navvies Huts, forming an encampment at the end of a tunnel, and surrounded by the 'Slough of Despond',

saturated with odour of all sorts. The huts are deadly cold in winter and hot in summer. There were no privies, no ash pits, no drains or sanitation of any sort. Small Pox was regular along with other equally deadly diseases and there was a high mortality rate among young children. Overflow from other privies and ash tips, plus household waste and human excrement, gets washed down on to the road, and being there diluted, makes vast puddles of such rottenness and corruption, too difficult to describe.' The coal owners believed the houses would only be temporary due to the pit soon being exhausted, thus allowing the makeshift houses to be demolished.

_1924 & 1925._

The Willie Pit Cottages situated between Annfield Plain and Catchgate. They are pictured prior to demolition, propped up with timber to prevent them tumbling over due to subsidence.

Richard Dixon Snr with his son Richard at Catchgate. The house shown was close to the rear of what later became the Police Houses at Catchgate. The Dixon family have traded in the area for many years in transport and motor vehicle spares.

Copley's Buildings at Catchgate.

Parkfield Terrace, Hare Law.

Feed the Children. This was probably taken during the strike of 1921 or '26 at East Pontop, Area No 7.

North Road, Catchgate showing the old Smith's Arms on the left and the Moor Pit in the distance. The Smith's Arms was built in 1860.

The underground toilets in Annfield Plain which closed down in 1917 due to a man falling down the steps. He died as a direct result of the fall. It is believed these old toilets were not removed for many years after this event. The shops in the background are now Cuthbertson Electricals and Lloyd's Bank.

A.H.&D. Cuthbertson Electricals. This family have traded in Annfield Plain for over 50 years. Their first shop was across the road in Front Street (once Thompson's) before they moved to their present shop. The family now also have a shop at Stanley.

Annfield Plain Council Offices at Hare Law.

A view of the crossing keeper's box at Stanhope & Tyne.

Northern bus on West Road pre 1920. This was one of the first service buses at West Road. Vehicle D24 was on route number 4, which was: Chester-le-Street-Stanley-Annfield Plain-Consett.

Tommy Gillingham with his beloved bus. Gillinghams have traded from Catchgate for many years. His wife Mary is one of the Dixon family mentioned below. Sadly Tommy died in recent years. He was very highly respected in the area. Mary still runs the shop and their sons have kept up the tradition with the buses from the garage behind the shop.

Mr Dixon with two of his buses at Catchgate. He also ran a paraffin home delivery service and at one time was in charge of the Empire Cinema at Stanley. He operated a bus service from Stanley to Dipton prior to the Venture Bus Co. Many will remember Dixon's Buses with great affection from the time he operated the late buses from Castle's Ballroom to Stanley and Consett. Mr Dixon also owned land at West Kyo and other places.

Trevor Howarth outside 'Instyle', Lady and Gents Hairdressing Shop, at Prospect Terrace, New Kyo. Trevor and his family have traded from this shop since June 1978. He and his family also have the 'Head Shed' at Stanley.

Durham Co-op Dairies at Annfield Plain Depot. Norma Harris is working at the milk carton machine in 1975.

William J. Callaway crowning the May Queen at East Pontop (Moor Pit).

A procession in Front Street for the 60th Jubilee of Queen Victoria in 1897.

The 1937 Coronation celebrations in and around the school yard at Annfield Plain.

West Kyo Coronation party in 1953.

A 1953 Coronation street party at Annfield Plain.

Walter Willson's, Annfield Plain, with the London Lending Library next door.

Kelley's bakery staff, Annfield Plain Bakery. Included are: Thomas Kelly Snr, Thomas Kelly Jnr, Peggy Robson, Jessie Ruddick, Susan Robson, Ada Kerswell, Mrs Bryson, Mary Peirson, Sybil Peirson, John Gillan, Andy Irwin, Jack Anderson and Tommy Brown.

Mrs Oxley and Evelyn Richardson outside Oxley's shop.

Joseph Oxley and his charabanc outside his shop.

Thomas Bainbridge, butcher, Catchgate.

Thomas Waugh with Anglo American Oil Cart at Catchgate, *circa* 1920.

The shop of T.&R. Lumley, West Road, Annfield Plain.

The delivery lorry of A. Wallace, Soft Drinks at East Terrace, Catchgate.

The blacksmiths at Catchgate: J. Irwin, D. Bulmer and R. Henderson.

Castle's Ballroom set up for a dinner dance. At one time, this ballroom was owned by Hindmarsh Enterprises who also owned Stanley Palais Dance Hall and the Royal Hotel at Whitby. Many will remember the 10 pm – 2 am dances on Friday nights, and dancing to the Tommy Smith Orchestra. Castles had a very good dance floor which often could be felt bouncing in the era of Rock 'n' Roll. At Bank Holiday weekends, the dance would be from 12 midnight until 4 am. Happy days and not a beer in sight.

Castle's Ballroom under demolition.

The Morrison Cottages, known locally as 'The Cements', at Annfield Plain. They were built for the miners and their families at the nearby Morrison North and South Pits. On the extreme left is the Masonic Hall.

Annfield Plain Co-op and the Corner House, once named the Railway Tavern or Inn.

Annfield Plain Co-operative Society

In 1870 there was a meeting of local residents of Annfield Plain and a few members from Tantobie Co-operative Society. A meeting of local people was then held in the home of Matthew Atkinson. After a few more meetings at this house, the decision was taken to form the new society. They rented their first shop to commence trading from Mr John Wright, a shoemaker from Kip Hill. The shop, where the Democratic Club now stands, had previously been rented by a grocer named James Brown. This shop opened for business on the 17th May 1870. The officials then were: Matthew Atkinson – president, William Eltringham – secretary and Thomas Luke – treasurer. At the first quarterly meeting on 9th July 1970 it was decided to purchase a horse for £3 10s and a dog for 9 shillings. It was also decided to enter as members of the Manchester Wholesale Society Ltd, thus affiliating them to the Co-op Wholesale Society which had only itself been in existence for six years. The Newcastle Society was formed in 1872.

In 1873, the building work was completed on their first purpose-built Central Premises which comprised of: grocery, provisions, drapery, shoes and hardware. Above the shops was the Co-op Hall which was used for society meetings, reading and educational facilities. Later, it was used for social events. In 1877, they opened a branch at Langley Park and also another at Dipton in 1880. Around 1891 more substantial premises were erected at Dipton due to much increased business. A third branch opened at Medomsley in 1889 and a fourth branch at Sacriston in 1897. Further branches were opened at Lanchester in 1907, Chopwell 1911 and Esh Winning 1914. According to *A Century of Cooperation, 1870-1970* by Sheila C. Forster, Annfield Plain Co–op also had branches at: Catchgate, New Kyo, Cornsay Colliery, Quebeck, Esh, Langley Park, Finings and Witton Gilbert. This book is in the Reference Section at Annfield Plain Library.

In 1896 the society purchased a large house and two lodges sited between the Annfield Plain School and the Co-op premises, and these were demolished so as to build a new drapery department. Also, old one storey dwellings, built in 1841 and known locally as 'Chippers' (owned by Ralph Fenwick), were demolished in 1896, and Strawbridges Buildings were erected on that site. These were later taken over by the Annfield Plain Co-op Society. The first built premises were later fitted with a glass covered veranda covering some of the footpath. The frontage was supported by iron columns, as was the drapery department. At this time, a dwelling house stood between the two shops.

In 1925, they erected a new block of shops adjacent to the first built premises and, upon opening, the veranda in front of the drapery department was taken down and used in the construction of the bandstands of Annfield Plain and Dipton Parks.

Mr A. Laws of the Co-op jewellery department.

An early photo of the greengrocery department.

The greengrocery department horse and delivery cart and driver on their rounds.

The Co-op butcher's cart and deliveryman. This horse was supposedly 35 years old! On 7th November 1968, a vote was taken to amalgamate with Dunelm Society and there was a 'Yes' vote of 125 with 25 against. In 1970, a meeting was held to decide on the suggested amalgamation with North Eastern Co-op and finally they decided to join up. At the final meeting in March 1970, it was decided 30 staff would be made redundant. The end of an era. Part of the Central Buildings of Annfield Plain Co-op Store was dismantled and rebuilt as a main feature in Beamish Museum.

A Co-op delivery man starting his round. The Co-op Dairy was situated behind the north side of Durham Road. It opened in 1932.

Annfield Plain Gleemen

The Gleemen pictured at one of their many concerts at Catchgate Methodist Church in the late 1950s. Included are: Pat Ogilvie, George Cairns, Bill Mumford, Harry Beckham, George Thomas, Bill Eaves, Tom Baker, Brian Ash, Harry Riley, Frank Connor, John Porter, Tot Gilbert, Alan Bell, Jack Stobbs, Joe Herdman, Norman Taylor, Gordon King, Eric Beckham, Bill Buglass, Bill Nelson, Bob Rowcroft, Joe Williams, Joe Middleton, Bill Eades, Sam Woods, Jim Speed, Albert Down, Pat Stobbs (choir accompanist), Jack Robinson, Bob Gilbert, Norman Crawford, Herbert Simpson, George Clayton, John Daly, Ted Hughes, Jack Wilson, Jack Bell, George Atkinson (artistes accompanist) and George Beckham (conductor).

In early 1903, local Annfield Plain Primitive Methodists, at the request of J.W. Glenwright, gave a concert at Dipton Wesleyan Church Hall. This led to the formation of a group of fourteen members, who practised weekly in Tom Turner's front room. They soon received many invitations for more concerts. The group were known locally as 'The Kyo Warblers'. After a few years, they gave a concert in the Primitive Methodist Sunday School Room, with their first president, Dr Cooke, in the chair. Guest appearances that first night were given by Miss Ella Bell, soprano, and Miss Maude Hunter, contralto.

In November 1906, the group evolved into a fully fledged Male Voice Choir. Tom Turner's front room was now too small for rehearsals, so they moved to the Odd Fellows Hall in Annfield Plain supposedly to an atmosphere of fried onions. Chris Mordue was the original conductor with Tom Turner the accompanist. Albert Laws was the secretary. Frank Allan became conductor followed by Maurice Pearce. After changing their name to Annfield Plain

Gleemen, Chris Mordue again became conductor

The most difficult years for the choir were the war years. Many members went away to the two world wars, and some did not return. However, those not called away, kept the choir going. In those early years, most of the members lived locally as do many of today's members. The choir competed in the Newcastle Festival and, as there was then little or no public transport, several of the members walked both ways, arriving home in the early hours of the morning after awaiting the result of the competition.

Over the years, the choir have performed in festivals and concerts throughout the land and have successfully competed against the best, seldom out of the first three. Blackpool and the Eistedfodd in Wales were two of their favourite events. They have also taken part in many annual celebrity concerts with such names as: Marion Nowakowski, Joan Hammond, Jennifer Vyvyan, Isobel Baillie, Ella Bird, Ralph Holmes, Owen Brannigan, Victoria Elliott, Ranken Bushby, Max Jaffa, Vernon and Maryetta Midgely, plus many of the local and national colliery bands.

The choir also ventured into Grand Opera when they performed in 'William Tell' at the Newcastle Theatre Royal and at Sadlers Wells. They have performed on stage, screen and radio and are the longest formed Male Voice Choir in the North of England.

Some of the former members were: Chris Mordue, Tom Turner, Edward Reay, Albert Laws, Harry Herdman, William Herdman, John Pearson, Jake Mordue, Joe Bainbridge, Sam Armstrong, Tom Brass, Ernie Carr, Robert Mitchell and Joe Gowland.

Most of this information is an extract from their 76th Anniversary account.

Accompanist for over 55 years, Patricia Stobbs.

Below is an account of the Gleemen since 1975 by Norman Taylor.

The choir has continued its aim of bringing the finest artistes to the area in its annual concerts. In recent years, Graeme Danby, a baritone born in Consett and educated at Greencroft Comprehensive School, has been a frequent visitor along with Valerie Reid, mezzo-soprano, who is now Graeme's wife. Graeme is principle bass at the English National Opera and, in 2003, when the choir celebrate its centenary, Graeme and Valerie are already booked as guest artistes. In 1983, the choir hosted the visit of Neukirchan Male Voice Choir from West Germany and, in September 1988, the Gleemen made a return visit to the same area. In 1992, the choir were honoured to sing for the visit of Prince Andrew at Durham County Hall on the 50th Anniversary of Aycliffe School. Another landmark at which the choir sang was at the Memorial Service, held at St Aidan's Church, Annfield Plain on the 23rd August 1997, for the 50th Anniversary of the Louisa Morrison Colliery Disaster. From 1997-2001, the Gleemen have fulfilled a contract to entertain SAGA Holidaymakers, performing a total of 55 concerts at Trevelyan College, Durham University and Henderson Hall at Newcastle University. The choir boasts an active membership of 45 voices. Musical Director, Norman Taylor, has been in charge for 32 years and their accompanist, Patricia Stobbs, has served the choir for over 55 years.

The Gleemen at Kyo Laws Methodist Church in 1976. Included are: John Daly, Bala Nair, Ray Newton, Chris Cain, Joe Herdman, Jack Cole, Jack Wilson, Mel Gardner, Robson Fewster, Jack Bell, Bob Fenwick, Alan Gibson, Dick Appleby, John Caldicott, Tom Ayer, Peter Conlin, Eric Wadge, Eric Tuckerman, Bill Hancock, George Thomas, Jack Curry, Dennis Dawson, Norman Crawford, Eric Beckham, Bob Rowcroft, Frank Connor, Albert Down, Colin Pearson, Pat Brinn, Ron Holden, Norman Taylor (conductor), Pat Stobbs (accompanist), George Cairns, Jamie Dickson and Roy Marshall.

James E. Glanville MP pictured outside the Houses of Parliament with his family, Bill and Alice Fawcett, and grandsons, Albert and Bill.

James E. Glanville, known all his life as Jimmy, was born in 1891 at Clavering Place (Wood Rows), Annfield Plain. He began work at the Morrison Colliery aged 12, and worked there for 40 years, mostly as a coal hewer. He became highly involved in the union and local politics.

In 1943 he became the Member of Parliament for the Consett Constituency which included Annfield Plain. He was elected unopposed due to wartime agreements, and replaced the late Mr David Adams MP.

After his selection, he was interviewed at his home at Grey Terrace. Oxhill. He pulled up his chair to the coal fire, lit his pipe, and reflected on his 40 years in the coal mines. He said, that moving to Parliament would not change Jimmy Glanville. He also stated, that when he went to the House of Commons, it would be in the same suit he wore when not working down the mine.

Local historian, Fred Wade, described Jimmy as going to Parliament as the Miners' Champion, and that he never forgot his mandate. He fought strongly on behalf of miners. On the day of his introduction to the House, he was escorted into the Chamber by fellow miners' MPs Lawson and Taylor. His Maiden Speech was in reply to an attack on the unions, and this caused quite a stir. He believed that a miner, or other worker, injured at work, should receive adequate compensation, instead of the lowly payment at the time. Jimmy was often in trouble with the Speaker, because he believed in speaking his mind.

In 1947, there was a disaster at the Morrison Colliery, resulting in the death of 22 miners underground. The day after, Jimmy attended a Relief Fund meeting. Speaking under the stress of great emotion, and with tears running down his cheeks, he said that many years previous, he had helped lay the underground road near where the disaster had occurred. He knew the hazards of mining, and personally knew most of those who had lost their lives, many since their infancy. He went on to say, 'Never let their memories fade, and never let their families want.' At this point he broke down, and asked to be excused from further speaking. Many of the women there, broke into tears at this point. Albert Fawcett, his grandson, told the author that Jimmy was so moved by this disaster, he went to his bank and withdrew his savings to donate to the Appeal Fund. Jimmy Glanville served the area he loved as MP until 1955 when he stood down. He was replaced by William Stones of Stanley. Jimmy died on the 19th September 1958, aged 67.

Annfield Plain Railway Station. The North Eastern Railway Co built a railway line from Newcastle to Consett. In 1893, the Annfield Plain Branch opened running north of Stanley and Oxhill. The line was opened to passengers as far as Annfield Plain in 1894 and on to Leadgate and Consett in 1896. Passenger services ceased in 1955 and goods ceased in 1964. This line remained open for traffic from Consett Steel Works until its closure in 1980 and then again a short while until it was finally removed. The organisation Sustrans then converted the line into a cycle track. Some bridges were removed but were replaced with more suitable new ones.

The crowd watch a loco de-railment between Oxhill and Annfield Plain.

Another photo of Annfield Plain Station.

This was the first motor lorry to displace the horse and cart delivery service at Annfield Plain Station. Pictured around 1936 is temporary driver, J. Collins.

Ransome & Marles

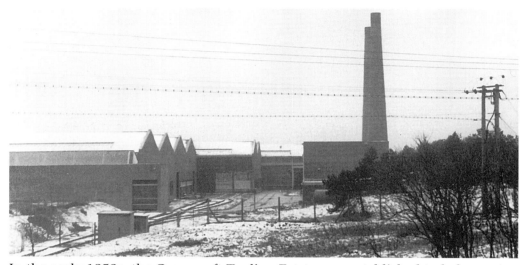

In the early 1950s, the Greencroft Trading Estate was established to help create work for people in the area due to the closure of local coalmines. The first factory on this site was that of Ransome & Marles of Newark. The factory was officially opened on Friday 1st October 1953 by Brigadier A.R. Lowe, the Parliamentary Secretary to the Ministry of Supply. The cost of the new factory was £400,000 and it covered an area of three and a half acres with space for extending another four times larger. The 240 guests at the opening were each given an inscribed bearing, made at Greencroft, as a souvenir. The staff were given a free meal and a bottle of beer. The first manager was Mr F. Graham and 90% of the workforce were local people. In those early years they produced 20,000 bearings per week. Within 10 years, the plant was enlarged three times, the largest of which opened in December 1963. The major contractor was Derek Crouch of Birtley. The Managing Director, Mr C. Richardson CBE, said, 'Our faith in the quality of workmanship in the North East, is surely proved by the fact that in the ten years since we started our Durham project, both the factory area and the labour force have been increased by 300%.'

The factory later changed its name to Ransome, Hoffman & Pollard, and sadly, for all its success, the work was transferred to the Newark factory where it first came from. Some say the decision was political. Who knows? One thing was certain, no matter how good and loyal the workforce were, in the end, it counted for nothing. Maybe it was that the car producers that were expected to come to the North East, just did not come until it was too late.

Ransome & Marles Bearing Factory.

The official opening of Ransome & Marles, 8th October 1953.

Men displaying their work on the day of the opening at Ransome & Marles.

The Juvenile Jazz Bands, South Moor Modernaires and Stanley Foresters, at the RHP Welfare Sports Day.

The demolition of the Ransome & Marles chimneys in the 1990s.

Annfield Plain Library
by Alan Harrison

The building of Annfield Plain Library was made possible by the donation of £3,000 from the industrialist and philanthropist Andrew Carnegie. Other monies raised were £300 from public subscription via: the coal owners, the Co-operative Society, councillors and other local people. The site was purchased for £50 from Mr J.T. Castle, and construction began in early 1908. The architect was Edward Cradney of Wallsend and the builders were local contractors, Messrs, W. Johnson & R. Southern.

The library opened on the 16th December 1908. A stock of 2,500 volumes was shelved, and the Lending Department opened in September of 1909. Mr Thomas Walker, a noted musician, borrowed the first book, Buchanan's 'Come live with me, and be my love'.

A Literary and Debating Society was formed in 1911, and during the First World War, part of the premises were used as a Recruitment Station and Food Office. A gift of £300 by the Miners' Lodges of Pontop, South Pontop, East Pontop and South Derwent, enabled the library to fund and stock a Children's Room which opened on the 17th December 1927.

Andrew Carnegie.

The Children's Room at the library. In 1946, a Library outing to Belsay needed 10 buses and 9 cars to transport the 360 people who went on the day trip. In 1942, the Naturalists Society was inaugurated, incorporating talks and summer rambles. In 1941, a sub branch of the library was opened in Dipton, prior to this there was a small library in the Collierley School until 1926. Annfield Plain Library was the first to be opened by an Urban Council in the Counties of Northumberland and Durham.

Mr J.W. Lawson who served this library from 1908 until he retired in 1950.

CHURCHES

Annfield Plain Salvation Army Band in 1924.

Kyo Laws Methodist Church. This church is adjacent to Annfield Plain Secondary School (the Uppers). Land was purchased from the South Moor Coal Co. The Conveyance of 29th February 1904 was for an area of land 1,078 square yards costing £202 2s 6d. The trustees were: J. Bainbridge, W. McClenning, J. Dunn, T. Milburn, J. Paxton, J. Walker, M. Armstrong, F. Manistre, B. Burridge, W. Johnson, H. Mudd, W. Kelly and Methodist Minister J.A. West. William Bell signed on behalf of the South Moor Coal Co.

The records in County Hall at Durham indicate church meetings were held in the Coronation Mission Hall at New Kyo in 1903. Even then there was talk of building a church. They could not decide for sometime which to build first, the chapel or the school. It was decided the cost should not exceed £1,050. They sought tenders for the building from July 1904. There was a delay until the contract was placed in 1905 with Mr Johnson of Consett at £500 for a Tin Chapel. The first sod was cut by Mr Pickering on 1st May 1905 and the Stone Laying Ceremony took place on 24th May 1905. The church opened in August 1905. At this time they vacated the Mission Hall premises in Coronation Street, New Kyo.

In 1941, the roof of Kyo Laws Church collapsed due to heavy snow. It was decided at a meeting on 9th April 1941 to close down as a church and to sell the building with members dispersed to other local churches. During this period, services had been held in the nearby Miners' Hall. The government requisitioned the old church and land, demolished the church, and erected a boiler house for Bevin Boys who were housed in nearby huts.

In 1954, the land and boiler house were handed back to the Trustees of the Kyo Laws Church Society in lieu of compensation. The boiler house was converted back into a church with money raised from the sale of scrap metal left on the site. Most of the work was carried out by the members. This church is still open today.

Kyo Laws Manse. Now the home of Mr & Mrs A. Dixon.

The Stanley Forum Gospel Group at Kyo Laws Church. Included: E. McMillan, R. Fenwick, E. Beckham, A. Wilkinson, T. Ayer, J. Cole and the Rev G. Kemp.

New Kyo United Free Methodist Church. The church opened in 1905 next to Cement Rows which were built to house miners from the Morrison Colliery. There is very little information available on this church although the Records Office do hold a list of baptisms. The church closed in 1937. The building was purchased and modified for use as the Annfield Plain Masonic Lodge.

St Teresa's Church. This Catholic church was opened and blessed by the Bishop of Hexham & Newcastle, the Right Reverend Monsignor Joseph McCormack, on the 17th December 1953. The church and presbytery cost £8,471. The church is built of red brick with red tile roof and seats 200.

St Aidan's Parish Church, Annfield Plain.

The flag or standard of St Aidan's Mothers' Union. In 1894, St Thomas' Church, Hare Law, was the Parish Church for Collierley, which included Annfield Plain. In 1898, a small Mission Church was erected at Annfield Plain behind the Tin School in Durham Road. The Parish of Annfield Plain was formed in 1912 as a separate parish with its own vicar. During these years services and baptisms had been held in the Mission Rooms. The foundation stone for the new church was laid on 25th July 1928 and was opened by the Bishop of Durham in 1929. The designs for the church were by Hicks & Charlesworth of Newcastle and the builders were, J. Jackson & Son. It is a plain brick building consisting of nave, chancel and vestry and is cruciform in shape. It has an outside bellcote with one bell. The vicar in 1929 was the Rev T. Dick. The present vicar is the Rev G. Laws who is also responsible for St Thomas' Church at Hare Law.

Jean Oliver, branch leader, and Olga Baxter, oldest member, cutting the cake in St Aidan's to celebrate 125 years of World Wide Mothers' Union, September 2001.

Annfield Plain Central Methodist Church.

The Girls' Life Brigade outside Annfield Plain Central Methodist Church in 1946.

The first Primitive Methodist Church in Annfield Plain opened in 1839 seating only 50 people in a small church in Front Street. This site was later occupied by Thompson's Stores. Two cottages had been knocked into one to form the church costing £81. In 1866 there was subsidence and the roof leaked badly. At this time they considered plans for a new church. However, the roof was raised on this building and a gallery was added increasing the seating to 200 causing a debt of £438. In 1895, Mr Fairley, of South Moor Coal Co, donated 960 square yards on the present site for a new church. This church opened in October 1896 and the total cost was £2,543 17s 5d. The caretaker's house was built in 1910 costing £224. The final debt was cleared by October 1913. There was a 50th anniversary in 1946.

In March 1993, a 17-year-old local girl broke into the church and caused a fire which almost totally destroyed the building. This created great distress to the members and most of the church records and Boys' Brigade equipment were lost. After the initial shock, it was decided to rebuild the church. I personally attended a Thanksgiving Service held outdoors. With night fast approaching, and heavy snow falling, over 60 people attended to hear the Rev Arnold Wright talk of a new beginning. After several hymns, the final one was, 'Will Your Anchor Hold In the Storm Of Life'. For this church, the answer to this question was a resounding 'Yes'. Building work was delayed by bad weather, and during this time of forced closure, services were held at the nearby St Aidan's Church. There was a re-opening and Dedication Service for the new church on Saturday 5th November 1994, at which I attended. The church was filled to capacity with representatives from all the local churches. This church has recovered where many others may well have folded thanks to those in charge and the church members.

Inside Annfield Plain Central Methodist Church before a fire. Note the Morrison Colliery Banner.

Annfield Plain Central Methodist Church under re-construction.

Annfield Plain Central Methodist Church after re-opening.

PC Ian Ward, with the Resurrection Cross of the Central Methodist Church. Many people visited the site of the burnt out church. One of them was Stanley policeman, Ian Ward. As he saw the sheer destruction, he decided to do something positive, rather than dwell on the past. He collected items from among the rubble. His hobby was wood turning and from a piece of charred wood from the pulpit, and a few nails from the roof beams, he constructed a cross which was named 'Resurrection'. This cross was used during the temporary services held at St Aidan's and was seen as a sign of continuity between the old church, and the one under construction. Ian also made a limited edition (ten) of copies of the Resurrection crosses for sale, to raise money toward the Building Fund. He also made and sold wooden jewellery, bowls and vases. Ebony keys from the destroyed Steinberg piano were also transformed into momentoes. This simple cross made by PC Ward in his home workshop became a symbol of hope and faith in the future of the church.

The former Wesleyan Church (St John's) with Mr F. Welch, Miss Welch, Mrs Cooke, Miss Lee, Miss Simpson, Mr Cooke and Mr Lee. Services were held in homes around the area from the 1830s. The Wesleyans obtained a site for a church next to the  newly built Pontop Rows around 1838. The brick built church opened in 1854. This church was later rebuilt and enlarged but coal workings subsidence caused the foundations to give way. After receiving compensation from the coal owners, they built a new church costing £720 and this church opened in 1870. A minister was appointed in 1880. From 1861-1881, the population in the village trebled and it was decided to build a schoolroom which opened in 1887. In 1896, due to overcrowding, they decided to build yet another new, larger, amphi-theatre type church.

The wooden towers were replaced by stone battlements in 1929. At the time of Methodist Union in 1932, they changed the name from 'The Wesleyan Methodist Church' to 'St John's Methodist Church'.

This church closed in 1963 at which time the members joined with the Methodist Free Church at nearby Catchgate, next to the Library. The Light of the World window from St John's was removed and refitted into the Catchgate Methodist Church.

The Wesleyan Church. Note the stone battlement.

St John's (Wesleyan) Methodist Church.

The view down to the Wesleyan Church.

Catchgate United Free Methodist Church. This is believed to be the huge crowd gathered for the opening of the new church. In the Catchgate area, the United Free Methodists built a Tin Chapel in 1873, just above Blackett Street. A newer larger church was soon needed and a site was acquired next to what is now Annfield Plain Library. This new church was opened by Mrs Dryden of Newcastle in 1903. She opened the doors of the new church with a gold key presented to her by Mr A. Davis. A crowd of over 600 attended the opening ceremony. The old Tin Chapel was sold to the West Stanley Liberal Club after being rejected by HM Commissioners of Works for use as a Labour Exchange. There was a Golden Jubilee Service held in 1953.

The Primary and Beginners Section of Catchgate Methodist Church in 1953.

The Junior Section of Catchgate Methodists in 1953.

The Ladies' Section of Catchgate Methodists, September 1978.

Catchgate United Free Methodist Church in 1953.

The 90th Anniversary of Catchgate Methodist Church in 1993.

St Thomas' (Collierley) Parish Church, Hare Law.

St Thomas'. On the 15th September 1840, the foundation stone was laid by John Clavering Esq of Greencroft for the new Collierley Parish Church at Hare Law, to be dedicated to St Thomas. Three coins from the reign of Queen Victoria were deposited in the stonework below ground level. This church opened on the 25th July 1841. Lanchester Parish divided on 7th July 1842 and the Rev Jackson received notice there was to be a new Parish to St Thomas, Hare Law, consisting of, Collierley, Kyo, Billinside and part of the parish of Greencroft. On the 1st January 1853, part of the church was destroyed in a gale. The belfry was blown down causing great damage. The church organ was installed in 1885. In 1929, a Mission Hall was erected at Greencroft and in 1930, a Mission Room was built at West Kyo. A Church Institute was built at Catchgate Road Ends in 1929. The Church Parsonage was built in 1858 costing £1,158. The centenary was held in August 1941. The rector in 2002 is the Rev G. Laws. It is known that the great grandparents of Hilary Rodham Clinton, wife of former US President Clinton, were married in this church.

St Thomas'
Chapel of Rest.

Dipton St Patrick's RC Church. Even though this church is situated at Hare Law, most local people refer to it as Dipton St Patrick's. For this reason, the story of this church will be included in the book *Dipton Remembered* by the same author. However, I thought it appropriate to include a photograph in this book.

Greencroft Primitive Methodist Church. In 1870, there were approximately 50 houses in Greencroft Village. A chapel was formed in a house at 4 Long Brick Rows in the downstairs room. This room measured 6 yards by 6 yards and was fitted with a pulpit in the corner of the room. It also had a 'singing pew' which held 7 people. There were several long wooden forms

for the congregation seats. Some of the members of this church broke away to form the United Free Church. They moved to a room at the north of the village. This group then applied to the Greencroft Estates for land for a new church. However, the Estates Office preferred to assist the existing Primitive Methodists, and granted a site to them instead. Money was borrowed interest free from local man Mr Reay, and the foundations were dug out by the members. The stones were quarried by Mr Elliott and Mr Plews. This stone was then carted to the site by Pontop Colliery coal carts, thanks to the manager, Mr Mitchieson. The builders were: brickwork by Mr Johnson and woodwork by Mr Mordue. The Foundation Stone was laid in 1888 and this church officially opened in March 1889 at Old Greencroft. This church was always well known for its choir. In 1898, membership dropped severely and there was talk of closure. In 1902, the church was badly affected by pit falls and some 50 loads of ballast were tipped into the huge hole. In 1910, Mr Ritson donated a new site. However, this was sold in 1928 and, the following year, plans were submitted for a new church. The church was built by Mr Rendle at a cost of £2,685. The church opened in November 1930. In 1943, the Boys' Brigade was formed. Such was the fame of the choir, the church was known as 'The Singing Chapel'. On the 23rd August 1947, church member Tom Bell was sadly killed in the Louisa Morrison Colliery Disaster when 22 miners lost their lives in an underground explosion. By 1967, membership had dwindled, and also during that year, rot was discovered in the roof of the church. A meeting was called and, with great sadness, it was decided the cost of the repair was too great. A decision to close was made. At Christmas 1967, they held a Carol Service, and Mr Philip Robinson sang 'The Holy City'. The last service was held on the 24th August 1968. The site was gifted to Annfield Plain Central Methodists. The balance of £1,054 was gifted to the Manchester Church Investment Fund, with a further £80 gifted to Annfield Plain, Catchgate and the Methodist Circuit. Lesley Armin was the last child baptised in this church.

Annfield Plain Salvation Army

General Booth, founder of the Salvation Army, visiting the Barracks at Annfield Plain in 1911. The first Salvation Army services in the area were held at the Tallow Factory at South Pontop (Greencroft) in 1888. The first captain was Miss Rushton who later married Mr H. Greener. In 1900, the South Pontop Coal Co needed this building back to convert into dwellings, so the Army built and opened barracks in 1901 on a site

between Annfield Plain and Catchgate. In 1920, they erected a larger building on the same site. General Both visited the area in 1911, the year before his death. This building is now a Tyre Repair Centre.

A group of Salvation Army members in 1934.

COLLIERIES

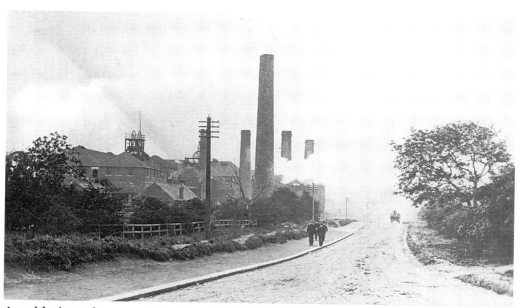

An old view along past the Morrison North Pit. The Morrison North & South Collieries were sunk in 1868. The Morrison East & West Collieries were sunk in 1923.

The Morrison North & South Pits.

The Morrison North Pit in the 1920s.

The Morrison Busty Lodge Band and Banner at the New Kyo Miners' Institute.

The entrance to the Morrison Busty Pit. Now used by Derwentside District Council.

The Morrison Busty Colliery, *circa* 1925, with the lamp room on the left.

A general view of the Morrison Busty.

A Ruston & Hornsby diesel locomotive underground at the Morrison Busty in the 1950s.

A coal plough in the Busty in 1947.

The Memorial Stone in St Aidan's Church Grounds. This memorial was laid in memory of the 22 miners who lost their lives in the 1947 Louisa Morrison Disaster. The stone was laid 50 years to the day of the disaster on 23rd August 1997.

In 1947, Nationalisation of the Coalmines took place on 1st January. The Louisa Colliery at Stanley, the William Pit at Old South Moor and the Morrison North Pit worked between them the area known as the 'Fourth North District'. This district had a history of flooding, and had only been re-opened that year. A problem was identified in so much as, the three collieries had differing arrangements. For example, due to an underground fire in 1929 in a section of the Low Main, the area was classified as a 'Safety Lamp Area', even though the fire had been contained by a sturdy brick wall. On the other hand, the Morrison North was classed as a 'Non Gassy, open light pit'. To create the same conditions for all, the men working in that district were all brought under Louisa Management and the Miners Louisa Lodge, and classed as a gassy pit area (no naked lights). On the night of 22nd August 1947, 24 men had been brought in for progress work, and to tidy up in the Fourth North District. Two men went down at 7 pm by the Louisa Shaft, namely Johnson and Kilgallon. The remainder descended by way of the North Pit. Deputies Hebden and Estell did their handover at the surface. Sadly, Estell had only just arrived in the district at 11.55 pm when an explosion ripped its way through the pit with terrible consequences. The cause of the explosion was that firedamp from below the Hutton Seam created an inflammable mixture of firedamp and air which was ignited by the illegal striking of a match to light a cigarette, shortly before midnight. This created a very mild firedamp explosion. However, due to widespread coal dust throughout the old and present workings, this small explosion grew in strength as it travelled around the area and resulted in the death of 22 miners. Two of those killed were Bevin Boys.

Bevin Boys at the Morrison.

A newspaper cutting of the 1947 Morrison Disaster. On Saturday 23rd August 1997, there was a Memorial Service at St Aidan's Church Annfield Plain, with Dr David Jenkins, former Bishop of Durham and clergy from throughout the area in attendance. A Memorial Stone was placed in the grounds of St Aidan's Church, only a short distance from where the dead and injured had been brought to the surface 50 years earlier. I can still hear the Annfield Plain Gleemen's rendition of 'The Lord's Prayer' and 'A Miner's Dream of Home'. A moving moment in all our lives.

RELATIVES and others wait at the gates of Morrison North Pit, Annfield Plain, for news of to-day's disaster. BELOW. Tired after recovering some of the bodies of the victims, rescue workers take a breather.

Pit Explosion: Fumes Hamper Rescuers

The four heroes of the Morrison Disaster in 1947 went to Buckingham Palace to receive their well earned Edward Medals with their families. The four men, left to right were: John Hutchinson,

Harry Robinson, Stan Shanley and William Younger. They had risked their own lives without thought of their own safety during the rescue.

Driver Albert Millions and fireman W. Moffatt in steam loco No 3, 'Twizel' at the Morrison in 1969.

The Lizzie Pit Band and Banner and supporters marching through Durham on Big Meeting Day. On the banner is Ramsey MacDonald with the Regulation Bill. This lodge closed in 1932.

South Pontop miners at the Lizzie Pit, Annfield Plain.

Section Four

Schools

A group of pupils from Catchgate School at St Thomas' Church for a Nativity.

Catchgate School

The old Tin School at Catchgate. This school for Mixed and Infants opened in 1879.

A class photograph of Catchgate School.

An early photograph of the Girls' Department in Catchgate School Yard.

An aerial picture of Catchgate School. The school opened in 1914. Note the prefab houses opposite the caretaker's house. These were built as temporary accommodation after the Second World War. They were later demolished to make way for modern housing.

The old Catchgate Junior School just before closure in 2001.

The building of the new Catchgate School in 2001. After the work was completed, this excellent new school opened for business on the 5th November 2001 to cater for 310 pupils. The last three head teachers have been: Mr Billy Bell, Eva Kay and present incumbent Ken Joel. This school boasts its very own swimming pool, and can you imagine how many thousands of children have benefited from this great learning facility. The swimming pool has been of invaluable help to other schools during the past few years after the unfortunate closure of Stanley Baths.

The staff of Catchgate School in the Millennium Year, 2000. Back row: Christine Falconer (class teacher), Jean Hird (class teacher), Lynne Fenwick (LSA), Dawn McDermott (nursery nurse), Alison Stafford, (classroom superintendent), Tess McTiernan (teacher), Joan McMahon (LSA), Middle row: Catherine Welsh (LSA), Pat Young (LSA), Mary Atkinson (supply teacher), John McDonald (class teacher), Julie McDonald (class teacher), Margaret Richards (return to learn), Sheila Patterson (supply nursery teacher), Sam Johnson (LSA), Margaret Ridley (classroom superintendent), Front row: Pat Riddell (class teacher), Jill Holroyd (class teacher), John Young (deputy head teacher), Mavis Crawford (secretary), Ken Joel (head teacher), Shirley Duggan (class teacher), Audrey Turnell (class teacher), Janice Allan (class teacher) and Kathleen Clasper (class teacher).

The Upper Standards School (Annfield Plain Secondary). This school opened in 1914, and the Oxford Exams were introduced in 1924.

Annfield Plain Secondary School.

Teachers at the Upper Standards in 1930/31. Included are: Angus Robert, Charles Urwin, Henry Knaggs, T. Nightingale, Eleanor Leathard, William (Titchie) Dawson, Henry (Basher) Boggan, Miles Hawthorn, Esther Jackson, Anthony Bolam (head teacher) and Nancy Smurthwaite.

The former Upper Standards in 2001 in a state of dereliction due to vandalism.

Ken Thomas, Demolition Contractors, demolishing the Uppers (Greencroft Lower School) in January 2002. It is believed a new housing estate will be erected on this site.

Annfield Plain Infants School

The demolition of Annfield Plain Infants School (Tin School) on Durham Road. This school was first opened in 1897 and the first head teacher was Miss Green.

The staff in the newly built Annfield Plain Infants School in 1974.

The staff at Annfield Plain Infants School in 2001. Back row: G. Iveson, J. Cruise, A. Chetter, S. Peacock. Front row: J. Roe, H. Wilson (deputy head), S. Marr (head teacher), D. Thompson and A. Mcloughlin. This school opened in September 1974 to replace the old Tin School. There have been three head teachers since it opened: Miss Hall, Mrs Hind and the present head, Mrs Marr. On the register in January 2002 were 125 pupils.

An old photograph of staff and pupils at West Kyo School.

West Kyo Board School. It is shown boarded up, probably due to closure.

Early staff at Kyo Kaws School (Annfield Plain). Included are: Miss Cruddas, E. Atkinson, ? Tweddle, J. Watt, ? Embleton, J. Tweddle, ? Dixon, H. Tweddle, ? Atkinson, L. Atkinson, W. Murray, Mrs Gatiss, W. Nattrass, J. Embleton and Mrs Smith.

Mr Seccombe at Annfield Plain School during Road Safety Week.

The staff at Annfield Plain Junior School in 1986. Included are: Ann Jordan, Howard Underwood, Mrs Joan Dixon, Jane McCormick, Lynne Tullett (deputy head), Alan Jensen (head teacher), Elizabeth Bartlett, Dawn Taylor. The last three head teachers have been: M, Golightly (1st September 1969), Alan Jensen (1st September 1982) and Lynne Tullett (1st September 2000).

Annfield Plain Junior School Football Team, winners of the President's Trophy. Included are: Alan Batty, Peter Kileen, Lee Harrison, Stephen Reynolds, Scott Coates (captain), Kevin Turnbull, Alan Sidey, Lee Cariss, Lee Browell, Philip Brown, Darren Longstaff and Craig Hunn.

Hare Law School was opened in November 1962, by Councillor I. Bell, to serve the special needs of pupils aged 4–16 throughout North Durham. The head teachers to date have been: Mr Parkin, Mr Alderson, Anne Collin and present head Mr Eagle. His deputy head is Margaret Collins. At the time of writing, there are 130 pupils on the roll.

SPORT

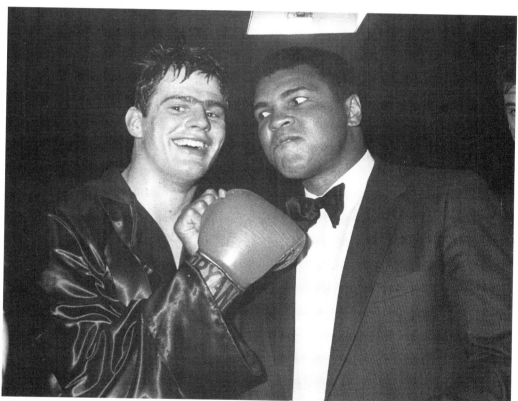

Glenn McCrory with the great man himself, Muhammad Ali.

'Gentleman' Glenn McCrory
Former World Cruiserweight Champion

Glenn George McCrory was born 23rd September 1964 in Burnhope. He was the third of a family of seven children: Gary, Karen, Glenn, Neil, David (deceased), Kelly and Shaun (twins). Glenn attended Dipton St Patrick's School before moving up to St Bede's at Lanchester. He was an all round sportsman at school representing them at football, running, long and high jump. At the age of 12, he joined Consett Amateur Boxing Club, and was coached and trained by Jonny Cuthbert and Tommy Gardiner. In 1981, he won an Outstanding Achievement Award for an 19 year old boy winning a Junior Championship. He fought and won an award while representing Young England against Germany in 1982. He was, 'Boxing News' Fighter of the Year' in 1989.

He won the World Cruiserweight Championship in June 1989 when his manager

Glenn McCrory – our very own World Champion.

was Beau Williford. Glenn actually sparred 100 rounds with Mike Tyson. He also fought Lennox Lewis for the British, Commonwealth and European Title. Since ending his boxing career, Glenn has become a member of the Boxing Writers' Club, and a journalist and broadcaster for Sky Sports since 1990. He has held an actors' Equity card since 1983. Glenn has had parts in 'Casualty', 'Spender', 'Quayside', 'Space Precinct' and 'Our Friends In The North'. He was awarded Ambassador of Derwentside in January 2000 and does work for the Sports Council, the Cancersports Aid Foundation and Derwentside District Council. At the present time Glenn has produced a song titled, 'We Will Stand', for a Children's Cancer Fund, which is dedicated to his nephew Greg McCrory who died of cancer on 12th December 2000, aged 16. Greg was the son of brother Gary. Glenn has also produced a play due to be performed at the Gala Theatre in Durham in August 2002 entitled *Carrying David*. It is the story of the relationship between Glenn's fight for the World Title and his handicapped brother David's fight for and struggle for life. Brother David died on 3rd February 1996, aged 29, of a muscle wasting disease.

Carrying David

Carrying David is a remarkable dramatisation of the McCrory family, as seen through the eyes of Glenn's foster brother David, severely handicapped with muscular dystrophy. Not expected to survive to fourteen, he defied all medical convention to enjoy life until he died at twenty nine. Powerless to move or speak through this unforgiving disease, he brought incredible love and joy into the lives of everyone he touched.

Glenn and David were spiritually as one and whilst Glenn physically carried him as a young man, it was David's immense courage, humour and determination to live, that inspired Glenn to become World Champion. David's influence still continues to drive the McCrory family from beyond the grave emotionally, such is the effect he has had on their lives.

The production, *Carrying David* will use the best of North East talent, including a choir

and brass band to produce exciting, entertaining and stimulating theatre. More importantly it gives a revealing profile of muscle wasting diseases. The play gives David a voice to shout on behalf of all sufferers and their families, so they can cope and retain hope. At the same time it affords an unique access into their world which, hitherto, remains only a dark secret.

Carrying David was written by Arthur McKenzie, ex CID Chief Inspector and script writer for 'The Bill', 'Casualty' and many other television, radio and stage plays. David McCrory is played by actor David Whittaker, who has worked extensively with the Royal Shakespeare Company. He has also appeared on television numerous times – including 'Spender' and 'Our Friends In The North'. Teddy Kiendl is the director and the play will also feature the music of Brendan Healy as well as a choir and a local brass band.

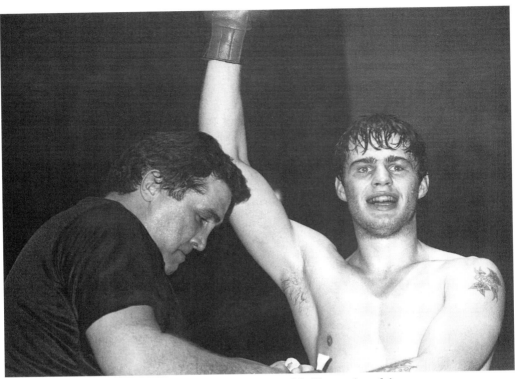

Glenn with his trainer after winning the World Championship.

Glenn in action. He was the undefeated British & Commonwealth Title holder.

The Glory of McCrory
by Michael Bailey

On Saturday night, the third of June,
The North East of England were 'Over The Moon'
It was a very special night,
Stanley was the venue of a World Title Fight.

The town had never witnessed such scenes,
Millionaires being chauffeured in their limousines.
Many stood outside, they had no cash, poor souls,
Like so many in the town, they were on the dole.

The District Council of Derwentside,
For hosting the event should feel great pride.
It was like a fairy story,
For the local cruiserweight, Glenn McCrory.

He didn't need any sort of mentor,
He was inspired by the crowd at the Louisa Centre.
As soon as they opened the dressing room doors,
He was almost deafened by the applause.

The preliminaries over, then the fight started,
This arena was no place for the feint hearted.
Very soon the crowd had high hopes,
When Glenn got Lumumba on the ropes.

He kept on scoring with left and right,
The crowd could sense that this was Glenn's night.
How Lumumba kept standing, we'll never know,
The crowd were now chanting 'Here we go, Here we go'.

When the final bell went, there was no doubt,
There was only one winner of this bout.
Some people were singing, some danced the Rumba,
They knew McCrory had beaten Pat Lumumba.

So let the Derwentside flag be proudly unfurled,
That's the home of, 'The Champion of the World'.

Annfield Plain Association Football Club

by Marshall Lawson, Secretary, Annfield Plain AFC

Annfield Plain Football Club was founded in 1890, and is one of the oldest clubs in the North of England, and a 'Full Member' of the Football Association. This club has the same voting capacity as the Football League Clubs in all FA matters. The ground was developed by supporters and local miners, who, in their spare time, laid 'tub rails' of carted ashes from the nearby Bankfoot Colliery to level the ground. This material was also used to create the banking around the pitch. The ground was originally known as 'The Fell', and one Saturday morning, it lived up to its name. The pitch caved in due to mining subsidence, and a cup tie with Bear Park was hurriedly cancelled. The club did not return to the ground until 1910. In 1921, new dressing rooms were erected with free bricks provided by the local colliery. In 1926, miners who were on strike erected the Old Stand. Robinson Bell, a founder member of the club, played in the early years, and he later became chairman. He and his family have provided strong links with the club over the years. Fred Watson from South Moor and Jack Peadon from White-le-Head were stalwarts behind the scenes, providing stability during a difficult period for the club in the mid 1970s.

The club joined the Northern Alliance League in 1902 after spending the earlier years in the Tyneside League. They competed in the Alliance League until 1925, winning the league title in seasons 1919-20 and 1922-23. The

Annfield Plain AFC, 1952-53. with the Durham County Challenge Cup. Back row: Dick Biggs, Bill Steele, Jack Wheatman, Pop Elliott, Tot Smith, Ray Scarr, ? Campbell, Miles Callaway (trainer). Front row: George Smith, Ken Harrison, Kevin Hewitson and Len Hubble.

Northern Alliance League disbanded in 1926 and the clubs moved into the North Eastern League, Second Division. Annfield Plain competed in this league until 1958. When the Football League Reserve Teams resigned from the North Eastern League to form their own competition it left the remaining non league teams to their own devices. Annfield Plain and West Stanley decided to apply for membership of the old Northern Alliance which had been reformed in 1935, whilst the remaining clubs moved into the Midland League.

Annfield Plain competed in the Northern Counties League from 1960-1962 and then rejoined the reformed North Eastern League from 1962-1964. This League was finally dissolved, and since 1964, Annfield have competed in the Wearside League. Over the years, Annfield Plain FC have fought their way to the 1st Round proper of the FA Cup in seasons 1927-28, 1928-29 and 1964-65. The 1927-28 season saw them drawn against another non league side, Chilton Athletic, who were Northern League Champions that season. The following year saw them entertain League club, Southport, and recorded an attendance of 7,200. The 1964-65 game saw them away to Southport who were a Third Division Club at that time. The club won the Durham Benevolent Bowl in seasons 1928-29 and 1934-35. In 1947, they won the North Eastern League Challenge Cup and then in 1952-53 they won the Durham Challenge Cup.

The later years have seen the club win the Wearside League in 1986-87 and 1997-98, and the Monkwearmouth Charity Cup in 1992-93. The post war years saw tremendous interest and support for the clubs in the area. Annfield Plain, West Stanley and Consett averaged crowds of 2-3,000, and the local derby games could attract 4-5,000. The North Eastern Challenge Cup Final between Annfield Plain and Consett was staged at West Stanley's Murray Park. The gates were closed an hour before the kick off time with 10,000 packed into the ground.

Annfield Plain AFC, 1981-82 season. Back row: Brian Rouse, Colin Carr, John Hooks, Colin Coulson, Derek Knowles, Ken Lindoe. Front row: Tom Kitto (trainer), Ken Walker, Stuart Bell, Keith Temperley, Stephen Lumley, John Carney, Andrew Spencer and Ralph Plumb.

The withdrawal of the League Reserve teams from the local competition, and then the decline of the mining industry, saw a decline in support during the '70s. The North Eastern League had always been a happy hunting ground for the League Club scouts, and during the period between the wars saw: Trevor Smith, Bob Heslop, Wallbanks, Grieve, and Mulcahy, to name but a few, leave Annfield Plain to sign for Football League Clubs. The period after the Second World War however, coincided with a succession of players leaving the club for higher spheres. Ken Smith to Blackpool for a North Eastern League record transfer fee. Jack Hather to Aberdeen. Andy Graver to Newcastle United. 'Jet' Saunders to Sheffield United. Maurice Morson to Blackburn Rovers. Bryce Ross to Carlisle. Charlie Weatherspoon to Sheffield United. Norman Wilkinson to York City. There are so many more that I could mention who have gone on to higher teams. Also, I am aware of the many people who have helped this club to survive over the years, too many to mention. It would take a separate book just for Annfield Plain Football Club. May I take this opportunity of thanking all who have helped in any way.

Annfield Plain AFC, 1984-85. Back row: Harris, Wood, Kennedy, Hedley, Turrell, Lindoe, Thompson. Front row: McCusker, Mullholland, Smith, Malone, Ward, Milburn, Tweddle and Bancroft.

Footnote by the author: At the time of writing, the football ground stand has been seriously vandalised, causing substantial damage. Over one hundred years of history almost wiped out in an act of wanton vandalism. A Charity Match was arranged including managers of Premier League teams, and players and former league players taking part in an endeavour to raise approx £6,000 to repair the stand.

The Morrison Heroes, 1919–20.

Catchgate School Football Team.

Annfield Plain Cricket Club

Annfield Plain Cricket Club at Burnhope, season 1958-59. Back row: Alwyn Sowden, Ron Elliott, Albert Brown, Brian Herdman, Bill Hall, Marshall Lawson, Tom Greener. Front row: Arthur Todd, Bill Gardner, Jim Sowden, Tom Richardson and Bill Whitfield.

Annfield Plain Cricket Club, 1963. Included are: P. Patterson, A. Greener, B. Gardiner, A. Todd, J. Jopling, G. Davison, B. Greener, B. McArdle, A. Whitfield, J. Carney and M. Bell.

Annfield Plain Cricket Club. Included are: N. Sherraton, J. Burrows,
B. Whitfield, J. Cool, T. Templey, A. Pattison, J. Graham, J. Stout, A. Brown,
A. Todd, B. Gardiner, R. Dodds, D. Dufton and scorer G. Thompson.

Annfield Plain Cricket Club, 1952. Included are: S. Barron, J. Cool, A. Welsh,
J. Burrows, J. Graham, G. Greenwood, W. Whitfield, A. Brown, A. Todd
(captain), W. Gardiner and A. Pattison.

Annfield Plain Cricket Club, 1946. Included are: J. Dent, N. Sheraton, R. Dodds, J. Burridge, R. Laybourne, T. Bell, T. McAllister (pro), B. Gardiner, J. Burrows (captain), M. Selway, J. Graham, T. Reynolds, J. Wilson, T. Sommerville and A. Todd.

St Thomas' Church Cricket Team, including the Rev Fisher Ferguson, 1924.

Annfield Plain cricket eleven and supporters.

Annfield Plain Park Bowling Green.

Annfield Plain Park Bowls Team, 1950.

Game on at the Plain.

Golf House, Annfield Plain. 4110

Annfield Plain Golf Course at top of Loud Hill.

Annfield Plain Park Tennis Team, 1959-60. Back row: Allistair Hunter, Brian Stafford, John Marsh, Dick Stansfield. Front row: Ray Pallister and Fred Stansfield holding the cup.

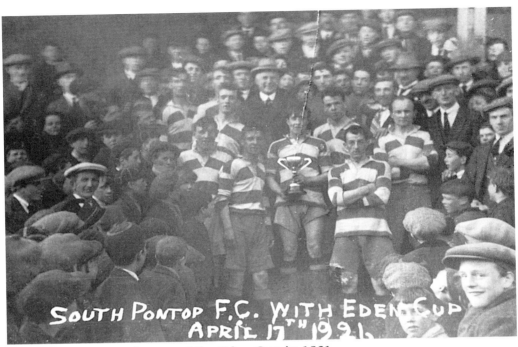

South Pontop FC, winners of the Eden Cup in 1921.

A presentation to Annfield Plain Cricket Team in 1964. They were winners of the League and Queen Elizabeth Cup.

Mick Horswill
FA Cup Winner with Sunderland AFC

Mick Horswill was born at Railway Gardens, Annfield Plain in 1953. He attended the local Tin School. When he was eight, the family moved to South Stanley and Mick went to Stanley Board School. He was encouraged in his football by Mr Seccombe. When he was eight years old, he was considered good enough to play in the Under 11s League against lads three years older than him. He was centre forward then. One problem he had was that he needed to wear spectacles. His mother Elsie solved that problem by taping his glasses to his ears. It obviously did not handicap him in any way.

Mick deep in thought.

He played in the school team and was an early cup medal winner. He later attended Shield Row School. While there he was captain of the Stanley and District Schoolboys XI. Mick was also interested in cricket and tennis. He signed schoolboy forms with Sunderland, and then for Sunderland Juniors. In July 1972, Mick was captain of the Sunderland Youth Team that won the Sanson Trophy in Chioggia, Italy. They beat Fiorentina, 1-0, in the Final. It was obvious he was talented when he began playing for Sunderland first team at the age of 16-17.

Receiving a cup in 1972 at Chioggia in Italy.

In 1973, Mick played for Sunderland at Wembley against Leeds United in the FA Cup Final and, as everyone knows, was on the winning side against all the odds. He was the youngest player on the field, but was not intimidated at all by the great occasion. Leeds were soon aware of his presence and hard tackling in midfield. This was his proudest day as a footballer, playing for the team he loved in the biggest game of all, the FA Cup, every schoolboy's dream.

After leaving Sunderland, Mick played for Manchester City, where he was plagued by injury. He then moved to Plymouth and Hull City, where he captained both teams, and Happy Valley, Hong Kong. He retired aged 32. He then managed several pubs.

Mick is still involved in local sport. He is involved with Sunderland Supporters Club (Annfield Plain Branch), Annfield Plain AFC and Annfield Plain

Cricket Club. He helps with the training of young local footballers and does a lot of charity work. His parents, Elsie and Eric, have encouraged him throughout his career, and even his grandmother never missed a local game. Mick Horswill was one of many local sportsmen from the area who went on to great things.

An inspiration to local youth.

Right: Mick, just before a game at Roker Park.

Below: Mick playing on the famous Wembley turf in the 1973 Cup Final. On the right is Ian Porterfield, scorer of the only goal which defeated the mighty Leeds United.

Norman Wilkinson

A great action shot of Norman Wilkinson going for goal while playing for Hull City against Bury. Norman was born in Alnwick in 1931, but moved as a young child to East Stanley, where he lived in Middle Street, then Noel Street. He attended East Stanley School before progressing to the Annfield Plain Upper Standards School. On leaving school, he began work as a cobbler at the Co-operative Boot Factory at Stanley. He worked there all his working life until 1967/8. His early football was with East Stanley Juniors.

East Stanley Juniors, *circa* 1947. Included: E. Jarmin, V. Henderson, A. Brown, N. Wilkinson (top left), George Lawson, H. Ashburn, J. Wigham, A. Gibson, G. Bird, A. Liddle, R. Gardner, S. French, J. Stobbs and H. North. At 17 years old Norman played one game for West Stanley, in the North Eastern League, as well as Stanley Rovers. At the age of 19, he signed for Annfield Plain AFC and played until he was 21, when he went into the RAF where he also played football. While there, Norman signed as an amateur for Hull City where he played in the 1st, 2nd and 3rd teams. In 1953, he was one of the servicemen who lined the route for the Queen's Coronation. At the end of his military service, toward the end of the 1954 season, Hull allowed him to sign for the last eight games for Annfield Plain AFC. In the summer of 1954, he signed for York City. Norman went on to be York all-time leading goal scorer with 143 League and cup goals in 402 appearances and is still thought of as one of, if not the best, players they ever had. Their best season was 1954-55 when they reached the FA Cup semi final. This is a list of their progress to the semi final.

> First Round: York City 3 Scarborough 2. Norman scored 1 goal.
> Second Round: Dorchester Town 2 York City 5. Norman scored 1.
> Third Round: Blackpool 0 York City 2.
> Fourth Round: Bishop Auckland 1 York City 3.
> Fifth Round: York City 3 Tottenham Hotspur 1. Norman scored 2.
> Sixth Round: Notts County 0 York City 1.

York met Newcastle United in the FA Cup semi finals. The first game was played at Hillsborough in Sheffield with a crowd of 65,000 and the score was 1-1. The replay was at Roker Park and Newcastle won 2-0 after a great fight by York City. The end of a dream. Some 247,916 had watched York's cup games that season. It is worth noting that Norman, at that time was only being paid £7 10s 0d a game, with a win bonus of £4 per game.

Right: Norman's (extreme right) first goal against Spurs.

Below right: Norman (extreme right) crowns a brilliant display with his second goal against Spurs.

Norman went on to play for York until 1966, aged 35. During all these years, he had always been a part-time footballer, while still doing a full-time job as a cobbler. From 1966, he played two seasons for Annfield Plain AFC and a further two years for Stanley RAFA aged 39. He is described in York City's Official

History as 'Without a doubt, one of the most loyal and outstanding players to ever appear for the club.' Norman Wilkinson, an outstanding player. Now retired, Norman still lives at Annfield Plain and likes to help out at the Plain.

Annfield Plain Homing Union (Pigeon Society) known as the Plain Club

The following is a summary of an account of the Society supplied by Jimmy Goodwin Jnr.

Prior to the introduction of long distance pigeon races, short distance racing was very popular. There were many small clubs around the local area. These short races over half a mile and one mile were over in minutes. Later, long distance pigeon races were introduced and it was a different set up altogether. Races were held over distances from 75-600 miles when the birds could be up to 16 hours on the wing. The Annfield Homing Union began in the early 1930s. Fanciers were from throughout the area including Lanchester, and Annfield Plain to Dipton. At the group's peak, there were 48 members and it was one of the largest clubs in the county. It was a well popular club and the members

Jimmy Goodwin Snr in 1952 winning the Channel Avge. At this time they had 30 members.

Jimmy Goodwin Snr and his famous B.P. Cock. His son, Jimmy Jnr, is shown holding the trophy at Jimmy's loft.

were very competitive. One of the older members suggests the club began at Annfield Plain Station. It is known the headquarters were at the Democratic Club with many great nights held there by the Pigeon Fanciers Fraternity.

Prior to 1950, the Annfield Plain Club were members of the Up North Combine, a large organisation with tens of thousands of members. In 1950, some of the clubs broke away from this large organisation to form the West Durham Amalgamation, including the Annfield Plain Club.

In the 1930s, '40s and '50s, money was scarce and pigeon racing was classed as a working man's sport. The birds had to be exercised and trained involving many modes of transport. Some would walk six or seven miles carrying their pigeons in a basket, while others would travel by bike, or with pram wheels, barrows or bogies, horse trap, public transport, or use local hauliers. Once at their destination, the birds would be released at a given point, 5, 10 or even up to 25 miles. More demanding training was done by way of British Rail, leaving from Annfield Plain Railway Station. The different baskets of pigeons were handed over to the porter, who in the 1950s was Hallie Goodrum. It then cost 2/6d for this service. The birds would be transported 50 miles or more and were liberated at a set time. Prior to the race, the birds were documented, fitted with a ring, and placed into large panniers along the station platform. The steam train would pull into the station and the birds loaded into a special carriage, ready for transportation to the designated station. The panniers of birds would again be lined up on the platform and released at the given time. Every Friday night, the members would meet at the Democratic Club to set their clocks and chat about the coming race over a few pints. They would meet again on the

Jimmy Goodwin Jnr. He has kept up the family tradition in the Homing Society, himself winning – 1st Club Annfield Plain, 1st Federation Annfield Plain, 1st West Durham Amalgamation 'Queen's Cup', 'Beauvais France' 410 miles 1997 birds WDA 10th June 2000.

Saturday night. The same things happened when the birds were sent to France for flights of 320-600 miles. The only difference being the birds were sent away on Tuesday or Wednesday from Annfield Plain to Folkestone or Dover by British Rail. Again they would be transported on to some other station in France, where the pigeons would be released by the station master. It was a great feeling to be at the station at Annfield Plain with all your friends in the club, seeing your birds on their way to the start of a race. Once classed the sport for the working man, now the sport of kings.

Every November the prizegiving was held at the Demi Club and there were some great nights. Meetings are now held at Catchgate RAOB Club. The following are but a few of the excellent results achieved by members of our club:

Ray Bell – 1959, tops the Combine from Amiens, France, 360 miles.
R Tate – 1976, Beauvais, France, 408 miles.
J. Flynn and Jimmy Goldborough – 1979, Appledore Inland National.
Ian Stafford – 1998, Bourgts, France, 559 miles, tops Combine.
Jimmy Goodwin – 2000, the Queen's Cup Race from Beauvais, in the Millennium Year, tops the Combine 1997 birds.
Walton & Lawson – 1973, Young Bird National, Letchworth.

Individual Top Flyers: Sayer, Thwaites, Staffy, A. Hall.

Some members old and new over the years: Andy Miller, Andy Pullman, Jimmy Goodwin Snr, John Hall, Andrew Hall, Ray Bell, Franky Barns, Ponto Dixon, P. Nixon, Geordie Craige, Alan Brown, Jimmy Goldsborough, Billy Sayers, Alan Crudice, Rafferty Bros, Colin Reed, John Johnson, Harry Robinson, G. Fisher, Jackson Bros, Gilbert McCrory and many others.

PUBS AND CLUBS

The present day staff of the Plainsman, January 2002.
Included are: Alan Roxy, Ruth Gray (landlady), Craig
Leonard, John Gray (landlord) and Tracy Graham.

Sandhole Workmen's Club. This club was first registered on 4th August 1905 in No 23 Grey Terrace, Sandhole. It is hard to believe that in those small premises in 1905 they had 335 members and in 1907 had 546 members. The secretary from 1905 until 1922 was Thomas Clark. In 1920 it was discovered the premises were suffering from mining subsidence and they submitted plans for the proposed conversion of a dwelling house, No 1 Hardy Terrace, and two houses and shops, Nos 2 & 3 Hardy Terrace, into club premises, with steward's dwelling house. This plan was approved and these premises were officially opened in August 1922 by Mr Stephen Clark of Stanley. The club included: ground floor, billiard room, sitting room and spacious bar. On the first floor was a large club room, games room, reading room and committee room. The alterations to the premises were carried out by Mr W. Ellender of South Moor from designs of J. Walton also of Stanley. The officials of the club at the time of opening the new premises were: chairman – W. Dixon, secretary – T. Gatiss and treasurer – F. Watson. At that time there were 400 members. Mr T. Gatiss was secretary from 1923 until 1937 when he was replaced by C. Hind who held the post until 1949. Up until 1962 the secretaries have been: W. Wright, J. Benfold, A. Farragher and M. Thompson. Some of the early stewards were: Mosey Turnbull, G. Dickinson and Frank Swales. The club has been upgraded several times and now has a modern bar and concert room. The club has a proud sporting history. The present officials are: secretary – P. Shotton, chairman – B. Carter and treasurer – T. Roe. The steward for the last three years has been D. Brown. The club had many successes in sporting events, including: the CIU National Whist Champions, 1932 and '33 and the CIU National Domino Champions, 1932 and '33. The present secretary, M.P. Shotton, has served this club for 23 years. The club have individual year books dating back to 1927. Club member M.H. Thompson has placed a time capsule behind bricks in the cellar of the club, not to be opened until after his death.

Sandhole Club, 1961. Included are: Alan Charlton, T. Hodgeson, J. Dixon, M. Thompson, Bell Watson, Matt Watson (steward and wife) E. Richardson, J. Johnson and others.

Officials, committee, steward and stewardess, Sandhole Club, 1982. Included are: Ronnie and Dorothy Ellies, M. Thompson, F. Curnick, J. Harman (secretary) M. Soulsby, P. Baines, A. Hardman, A. Charlton, D. Hardman, R. Bradburn, C. Williams, J. Yuill and J. Donaghie. Many officials and committee men have received awards for long service. They include: for ten years, J. Dixon, J. Johnson, J. Potts, J. Hardman, T. Coulson, M.P. Shotton, T. Roe, B. Carter, A. Charlton and M.H. Dennison. For 25 years: M.H. Thompson.

New Kyo Constitutional Club. New Year's Day in 1991 with a competition between the men and women in a charity darts match and a bit of cross dressing to make it more fun.

Fancy Dress Competition winner, Terry Snaith in 1986.

By its name, the New Kyo Constitutional Club obviously had a political background in the early days. According to Fred Wade, the first site of the club was just to the rear of Sycamore Terrace, New Kyo. It was formed in 1914 and the first steward was Matt Hardy. He was succeeded by Ed Wilson, T. Robinson, R. Martin, J. Jackson, G. Dodds and others. The first officials were: Tom Middlemass, Tom Howe and Tom Clark. A short time after opening, Tom Defty was elected chairman and he held this position (apart from two short breaks) until 1951. Jasper Dodds was also a long serving official, as treasurer, until 1950. Two other long serving officials were: Edward Graham and Jack Anderson as secretary. Three other well known officials were: Maurice Leonard, Bob Reay and Ed Clayton. The club stayed on this site until 1918, when they moved premises to the existing site.

The club has been known locally for many years as 'The Monkey' due to the gift of a stuffed monkey to the secretary of the time by a Leadgate trader. This was kept behind the bar for many years. Folklore suggests it was the original 'Monkey from Hartlepool'. Fishermen from there hung a monkey which had been washed ashore. They supposedly believed the monkey to be a French Spy. During later alterations to the club, the monkey was stored in the cellar and has not been seen since.

In the Burns Pit Disaster of 1909, when 168 men and boys lost their lives, 43 members from this club were among the dead. The club, with others, raised money for a memorial to the dead, and it presently stands in the entrance to Stanley Cemetery after being sited outside Stanley Council Offices for many years.

In 1950, the new extensions were opened. In more recent years, Ted Snaith and Ivan Bragan, have both been given well earned long service awards. The last structural alterations were in 1962 on the new downstairs lounge and bar. The Monkey club was the first in the area to have 'Professional Artists' for the entertainment. Though only a small club, they are noted throughout the district for their sporting achievements in football, cricket, darts, dominoes, whist and pool. At one time they had as many trophies behind the bar as Manchester United. The present day chairman is Ted Snaith.

Catchgate Excelsior Club & Institute in 2002.

An old picture found in the cellar of the Catchgate Excelsior Club & Institute of officials, committee, steward and wife.

Officials and committee in more recent years. Included are: W. Carter, W. Lowes, J. Gailes, K. Maddon, J. Little, G. Wakeley, B. Ridley, T. Wilson (secretary) and J. Stubbs (treasurer). As the original club records are no longer available, it is not exactly known when this club opened. However, Kelly's 1902 Directory lists the secretary of the club in that year as being Thomas W. Cunningham. The club joined the CIU on 17th August 1908. The present officials are: secretary – R. Stobbs, chairman – V. Little, treasurer – B. Southern. The steward, G. Hall, has been a loyal servant of the club over a period of 24 years. He has also worked in that capacity at South Stanley RAOB Club and the Crown & Thistle.

An old photograph of the Annfield Plain Democratic Club & Institute (the Demi). On 15th July 1902, plans submitted by Mr S. Wilkinson on behalf of Annfield Plain Democratic Club for the alteration and extension of premises in West Road were approved. This club was on the site that later became the Vic Club. The Demi traded here until 1905 when records show the new club in Front Street was first registered on 8th July 1905. The original opening hours were, 9 am-11 pm. It is believed the original Annfield Plain Co-operative Store was on this site prior to the building of the club. The secretaries of the club since 1905 until 1962 have been:

1905-1915 T. Burton   1915-1917 E. Snaith   1917-1921 T. Irwin
1921-1946 E. Snaith   1946-1962 George Lowery

In Kelly's Directory of 1902, the secretary was then Robert Ridley. The present officials on 1st January 2002 are: secretary – R. Thompson, chairman – R. Wardman and treasurer – G. Hall. The steward of the club at this time is Brian Raine.

The club in January 2002 also showing the Queen's Hotel.

Front Street, Annfield Plain, showing the Queen's Hotel. This public house was listed in Hagar's 1851 Directory, as 'The Queen Elizabeth Hotel'. It was originally a large double fronted house. There was a long sign, almost the length of the building, situated between the ground and first floor, reading: 'John Dodds, Wine & Spirit Merchants, Good Stabling.' There was a blacksmith's shop behind the hotel. The Queen's was later rebuilt in 1901 into the grandiose building it is today.

Bart Kelly pictured behind the bar of the Queen's, year not known. The present day owners are Jonathan and Margaret Graham.

The Stanhope & Tyne Railway (The Plainsman). This public house was erected around 1835 by Mr C. Allen who was a contractor for the embankments of the Stanhope & Tyne Railway. Mr Allen built a brewery and associated properties which comprised of: stables, a shed for the drays, plus five or six houses for the draymen and employees. Mr Allen also owned most of the land to the rear of the brewery plus more land to the east of Durham Road. His successor was Mr J. Lumley. The brewery closed in 1870. This was believed to be the only public house to take the name of that railway.

Here, the pub has changed its name to 'Winners'.

The present name is 'The Plainsman'. The current owners are John and Ruth Gray. This is a Blue Star house.

The former Smith's Arms at North Road, Catchgate. Shown in the photograph is a view along North Road with the Moor Pit in the distance. This pub was built around 1850 by Mr Nicholson Welch who then lived in the Toll House. He was also a blacksmith, hence the name. The pub was known for many years as Keheo's or Keo's.

Inside the Smith's Arms. Including: Hilda and Ernie Reader, Mrs Halliday, Billy (Happy) Halliday and Tommy Wall. In the background is Landlady Mrs Kehoe.

The Smith's Arms, Catchgate. The present owners for the last two years are George and Karen Dixon. They were, a few years ago, at the Coach & Horses at Annfield Plain. The manageress is Nan McGrandle. The modern day Smith's Arms is much grander than the old pub and also much larger. The two storey building on the left supposedly at one time included a butcher's shop.

The original building of the Coach & Horses, West Road, Annfield Plain.

This hotel was originally named the Railway Tavern. It has had several names including the Corner House. In Hagar's Directory of 1851 the landlord was Isabella Turnbull, and the hotel was also registered as a blacksmiths. It closed for some time but has now reopened as the Corner House and has regular discos with 'Peachy' as the DJ. The present owner is Mr Peter Graham.

Catchgate RAOB Club. This club was first formed as the Annfield Plain & Dipton RAOB and was registered as the Swinburne & Dipton Lodge. They paid £400 to purchase the colliery owner Mr Mitchison's house at North Road, Catchgate. It was a private club for one year before they applied to join the Club Union. The name changed in 1959 to the Catchgate RAOB Club and it was no longer compulsory to be a member of the Buffs Lodge to join the club. RAOB stands for the Royal Antediluvian Order of Buffaloes, an order that still exists today. Also in 1959, they obtained a mortgage from the Federation Breweries to erect a newer, larger club only yards behind the old club. In 2002, the officials are: chairman – Bobby Curtiss, treasurer – Jimmy Goddard and secretary – Cecil Robson. The present steward and his wife are Vic and Olive Kendall who have been loyal servants to this club.

RAOB Committee men and officials. Included are: Vince Proud, Frank King, Bob Curtiss, Jack Johnson (CIU), Eddie Proudfoot, Jack Lynam, Jim Hardman and Wilson Thirlaway at a long service awards ceremony.

The RAOB ladies' darts team. Included are: Monica Pryce, Eleanor Gilliead, Gina Hodgson, Betty Perryman, Jacky Lynch, Mrs Bandtock, Peggy Lizzie Hodgson, Diane Walton, Ina Ginty, Linda Wilson and Mrs Coleman.

Included in this group at the RAOB are: Harry Perryman, Norman Chamber, Bob Curtiss, Jim Goddard and Vince Proud at a fund raising event at the club.

The Green Tree, Catchgate. This old pub was sited west of the RAOB Club on the other side of the road. It was kept for many years by George Ridley as an off licence. Due to subsidence, it was shored up with timbers for many years, and was finally pulled down.

The Crown & Thistle, Catchgate. This is the oldest known pub in the area and the second of its name on the same site. The original deeds of this property go back to 1670 when it was a dwelling house. It was converted into the Crown & Thistle in 1817 and the landlord in 1851 was Joseph Irwin who was also listed as a joiner, cartwright. It was later rebuilt. The present day landlady is Lillian Ogden and she has been there some four and a half years.

Annfield Plain Gleemen at Stanley Civic Hall, May 1999. Included are: Mel Gardner, Ray Cooper, Jim Doonon, George Laycock, Robson Fewster, Alan Gibson, Alan Jamieson, Bill Stewart, Vince Lennon, Alf Brown, David Conlin, John Bailes, Tom Ayer, John Martindale, Ian Parker, Eddie Hughes, Bill Crinson, Bob Walker, Peter Charlton, Jack Stobbs, Terry Pinnegar, Tom Bailes, Ivan Stretton, Arthur Barnaby, Peter Conlin, Bob Thompson, Eric Wadge, Eric Beckham, Bob Rix, Brian Charlton, Jack Thompson, Bill Hancock, Dick Laycock, Dennis Dawson, Roy Marshall and Alan McRea. In the year 2002, the Gleemen have been going strong for 99 years thanks to the dedication and interest of so many like minded people with a love for music.

The People's History

To receive a catalogue of our latest titles send a large SAE to:

The People's History
Suite 1
Byron House
Seaham Grange Business Park
Seaham
County Durham
SR7 0PY

www.thepeopleshistory.com